# The Art of Man-Fishing

# The Art of Man-Fishing

## Thomas Boston

Introduction by
J I Packer

Christian Heritage

© 1998 Christian Focus Publications Ltd
ISBN 1 85792 106 2

Published by
Christian Focus Publications Ltd
Geanies House, Fearn, Ross-shire,
IV20 1TW, Scotland, Great Britain.

# Contents

# INTRODUCTION

## I

In January, 1699, 22-year old Thomas Boston, already a licensed preacher in the Church of Scotland though not yet a parish pastor, 'wrote a soliloquy on the art of man-fishing'. The soliloquy has the form of a sermonic meditation addressed to himself on Christ as his model for his ministry of the word. In the memoirs which Boston edited for his children in 1730, as his life neared its end, he recalled how it happened.

> 6th January 1699, reading in secret, my heart was touched with Matt. iv. 19, 'Follow me, and I will make you fishers of men.' My soul cried out for accomplishing of that to me, and I was very desirous to know how I might follow Christ, so as to become a fisher of men; and for my own instruction in that point, I addressed myself to the consideration of it in that manner.... That scribble gives an idea of the then temper of my spirit...[1]

The 'scribble', so Boston tells us, was never finished (not that it leaves any sense of incompleteness when read today), and no one outside the family saw it till it was published in 1773. Since then, however, it has been constantly hailed by evangelicals as a masterpiece on ministry, worthy

7

to stand on the same shelf as Baxter's *Reformed Pastor*, and it is in those terms that I commend it now.

The idea of a beginner preacher of 22 producing a spiritual masterpiece is startling, no doubt. But Boston was an unusual man. He had been brought up by godly, conscientious Presbyterian parents (as a child he had on one occasion accompanied his father to gaol for the latter's nonconformity). He had been soundly converted at age 11, through the ministry of Henry Erskine, a veteran saint in his sixties who had been one of the two thousand Puritan clergy ejected in 1662 and who during the winter of 1687 was minister of a church four miles from Boston's home. His father took him to hear Erskine, a spiritual impact was made immediately, and then 'in the winter, sometimes it was my lot to go alone, without so much as the benefit of a horse to carry me through Blackadder water, the wading whereof in sharp frosty weather I very well remember. But such things were then easy, for the benefit of the word, which came with power.'[2] 'Sure I am, I was in good earnest concerned for a saving interest in Jesus Christ; my soul went out after him, and the place of his feet was glorious in my eyes.'[3] He and two other Christian boys from his school 'met frequently in a chamber in my father's house, for prayer, reading the Scriptures, and spiritual conference; whereby we had some advantage, both in point of knowledge and tenderness.'[4] Boston's lifelong habits of self-scrutiny, prayer, and Bible reading with systematic meditation, were formed at that time.

There is more to be said. As Boston had a sensitive spirit, so he had a first-class mind, a retentive memory, and a way with words. He was always a man who thought best with a pen in his hands, writing out ideas and arguments as they came to him. He had matured early; his theological convictions were clear, his sense of call to a preaching and shepherding ministry was strong, and his insight into the vistas opened by biblical texts was already deep. The qualities that were later to lead Jonathan Edwards to describe him as 'a truly great divine' were already in evidence, and the power to speak to the heart that is sustained throughout his later and greater treatise, *The Fourfold State* (1720), was there too.

Put all of this together, and the star quality of *The Art of Man-Fishing*, while still breath-taking, becomes at least intelligible.

## II

Boston was a mainstream Scottish Puritan (to use the word that fits; 'Puritan' was not used in Scotland as a label in the way it was in England). The Puritan type of faith and piety received its classic formulation in the Westminster Confession and Catechisms, which were the authorised standards of the Church of Scotland in Boston's day. It will help us to appreciate the pastoral theology of the *Art* if we remind ourselves of the main features of the Puritan outlook, as the Westminster documents display them.

The Westminster standards were drawn up by the veritable cream of English and Scottish clergy. Working in the middle years of the 1640s, they had behind them as resources and models, establishing perimeters, parameters, and trajectories for their thought, the sixteenth century Reformed confessions, including the Anglican 39 Articles which they were charged to supersede; the legacy of theological exposition that began with Calvin and Knox; more than a century of intense international debate, carried on in print, regarding Roman Catholic, Lutheran and Arminian deviations from Reformed views; dozens of catechisms produced by Puritan pastors, and a great deal of catechising experience; much published exegetical and expository work on the biblical text, from both Catholic and Protestant scholars; and, last but not least, a mass of 'practical affectionate' English Puritan treatises on conversion and the inner devotional realities of the Christian life. Basic to Westminster's theological method was belief in the divinely inspired truth and coherence of the Bible, and a resolve to affirm only that which could be verified and vindicated from Scripture itself, as a faithful echo of God's own teaching. Drawing on the resources listed above, and hewing conscientiously at every point to the line of Scripture, Westminster theology was masterful in style as well as masterly in substance, and it is no wonder that it shaped Presbyterian and Reformed theology both sides of the Atlantic so decisively.

Westminster theology is trinitarian, and centres on the way in which mankind's Creator and Judge became mankind's Redeemer and Saviour through the outworking of a plan that casts Jesus Christ, the God-man, in the role of Mediator and the Holy Spirit, the Paraclete, in the role of the Life-giver. The plan is like an ellipse with two foci: focus one is the covenant of grace whereby, on the basis of Christ's righteousness and blood-shedding, relations between the Creator and his human creatures are restored; focus two is union with Christ by the Spirit in regeneration whereby fallen human nature is remade. In all of this the Lord Jesus Christ himself, God incarnate who redeemed, rose, reigns, and will one day return to judgement, becomes the direct object of faith, hope, love and joy. The world-wide church, of which all Christian congregations are members, is the sphere of salvation as it maintains the ministry of the word and sacraments and worships God according to his com-

mand. Christ is the Head of the church and through
the Spirit the source of all its spiritual life, and the
church must be the Christian's home as long as he
is in this world. Such in a nutshell is the theology
of Westminster.

Implicit, and sometimes explicit, in the Confession and Catechisms is the Puritan concept of
conversion as a process that begins with awakening from spiritual complacency to spiritual unease
as one faces the reality of one's sin, and leads on
through questings for faith, repentance, and a new
life with God, to a God-given confidence that one
has been divinely enabled to turn from sin to a self-
abandoning trust in Christ, the sin-bearer, as one's
Lover, Lord, and Life, and that one's heart has
been renewed in the process. Boston's idea of the
minister as a 'fisher of men' is that through his
public ministry in the pulpit and his private ministry of one-to-one admonition God will work in
people's hearts to bring them to this place of settled
commitment, where they can confirm their assur-
ance of being alive to God by noting the ongoing
change in their inner being.

Believing that the fallen human heart is desperately prone to optimistic self-deception, Westminster Puritans stressed the need for constant self-
suspicion and self-examination. There was nothing of morbid introspection about this; on the
contrary, it was experienced as a bracing and

reassuring exercise, as the regenerate discerned within themselves the signs of life from the Holy Spirit. Boston, facing the fact that only those alive in Christ can follow Christ, himself takes time in the early pages of the *Art* to examine himself in this way.

I think I have Spirit; that is, that I have life... from the following grounds... I have light that before I did not have.... This light lets me see my heart-sins... and is still discovering the baseness of my heart to me.... It makes me see Christ as precious... makes me trust in him... I lean on him for help in his own work... in temptations and trials, I endeavour to lift up my soul to him. I feel help... from the Spirit.... Many times I have gone to prayer very dead, and have come away with life... I find a threefold flame, though weak, in my heart. (a) A flame of love to Christ... I have a love to his truths... I love the promises... I love his threatenings as most just ... I love those in whom the image of God appears... I love his work... I love his ordinances... I love his glory, that he should be glorified, come of me what will. (b) I find in my heart a flame of desires toward the righteousness of Christ... My soul... acquiesces in justification by an imputed righteousness... Sometimes my soul longs... to be dissolved, and to be with Christ... (c) I find in my heart some heat of zeal for God... I move forward towards heaven... I am more acquainted with Christ and his ways than before... there is a growth of love in me... I can, I think, trust God more now than before... my soul is habitually more watchful than before. Nor do I dare give such liberty to my heart as sometimes I gave... I see growth of contempt of the

13

world. And this, blessed be God, is on the increase in me (pp. 50ff.).

Evangelism was not a word that Boston knew, but evangelism, in the sense of awakening the unconverted to their need of Christ, leading them to faith and repentance, and establishing them in the new life to which his own self-analysis testifies, is what 'man-fishing' meant to him, and it was this skill that he sought to learn from the example of Jesus' own soul-winning service.

### III

Puritan evangelism, as carried on by preaching and pastoral admonition, took time, and was expected to take time. Strong sudden impressions from God about particular spiritual issues would frequently occur as the word of God was preached, but ministers in the Westminster tradition were realistic about the likelihood that the conversion process from start to finish would take months, just as the gestation and final birth of a human baby does. In this, men like Boston have an important lesson to teach us today. Since mass evangelism on neutral ground, led by a freelance who specialises in this particular activity, became a regular feature of the Christian scene, the concept of conversion as typically a short, sharp affair that can be precisely narrated and dated has become normative for evan-

gelical minds. Clearly, its source is the evangelistic rally, where, after warming up and softening up
preliminaries, the evangelist speaks of human sin
and divine grace, appeals for commitment to Christ,
and passes on those persuaded to counsellors, who
help them to make their commitment firm. Our
romantic imaginations are right to recognise re-
ceiving Jesus Christ as Saviour from the guilt and
power of sin and Lord of one's life henceforth as
the essence of conversion, but wrong to fancy that
the whole process ordinarily starts and ends within
an hour or two; just as we are wrong to imagine, as
we sometimes do, that any happy results from the
rally depend in a decisive way on the evangelist's
special gifts and the quality of his performance.

Realism requires us to face the fact that though
God may prompt special evangelistic ventures,
and use them in a spectacular way to advance or
complete the conversion process, that process usu-
ally has many other stages, in all of which the
decisive factor is the sovereignty of God's grace.
The main way in which God advances conversion,
in our day as in Boston's, is through the sustained
faithfulness of parents, friends, and church teach-
ers witnessing, instructing, and encouraging infor-
mally, and of preachers expounding the gospel
from Scripture in worship contexts. The first re-
quirement, therefore, in the church's unending
work of 'man-fishing' is that these activities go on

incessantly, shaped by clear and serious purpose
and backed by earnest importunity in prayer.

## IV

Boston wrote the *Art* when he was a probationer
preacher looking forward to a life of parochial
ministry. Naturally, therefore, it was the demands,
problems, and pitfalls of his present and future role
that concerned him most, and the second half of the
work is taken up with exploring what following
Christ in faithful ministry involves. From this
standpoint, the *Art* is a classic text which any
minister of the word in any age might well use for
an annual check-up. Certainly, we who preach will
never get beyond its clear-sighted, challenging,
searching wisdom, of which the following is a
rough summary.

The call of God to shepherd his flock (says
Boston) requires us to model ourselves on Jesus
Christ, our Lord and Master, in at least the follow-
ing particulars:

1. *Faithfulness*, even when it runs the risk of
upsetting people and turning them against us. We
must renounce the 'carnal policy' of trimmers and
time-servers who tone God's message down, and
must present the realities of sin and grace forth-
rightly, rebuking where necessary, pulling no
punches, and leaving the outcome to God.

2. *Evangelistic purpose*. 'Christ had the good of souls in his eye.... When you preach, let this be your design, to seek to recover lost sheep ... to get some converted, and brought in to your Master.'

3. *Prayerfulness*. Christ spent time and energy in prayer both before and after his preaching of the word, and we need to do the same.

4. *Single-mindedness*, free from any form of the personal profit motive.

5. *Enterprise in usefulness*. Jesus took every opportunity 'to instruct, rebuke, etc., from such things as offered,' both one to one and in larger companies. So must we: so 'learn the heavenly chemistry of extracting some spiritual things out of earthly things,' and 'do not refuse any occasion of preaching when God calls you to it.' 'If Christ should come and find you idle, when he is calling you to work, how will you be able to look him in the face? They are well that die at Christ's work.' These are the last words of the book.

A century and a half after Boston's time, another Scotsman, Horatius Bonar, wrote a powerful hortatory hymn on Christian ministry which, whether he realised it or not, capsules perfectly the admonitions of Boston's *Art*. My guess (which of course I cannot prove) is that he knew his Boston so well that he could not think of ministry save in Bostonian terms. His hymn is certainly another admirable text for the minister's periodic self-assessment, and the best way to end this introduction will be to quote it in full. This, then, is what Boston's message to us amounts to.

> Go, labour on; spend and be spent;
>     Thy joy to do the Father's will;
> It is the way the Master went:
>     Should not the servant tread it still?
>
> Go, labour on while it is day;
>     The world's dark night is hastening on;
> Speed, speed thy work; cast sloth away;
>     It is not thus that souls are won.
>
> Men die in darkness at thy side,
>     Without a hope to cheer the tomb;
> Take up the torch and wave it wide,
>     The torch that lights time's thickest gloom.
>
> Toil on, faint not, keep watch, and pray;
>     Be wise the erring soul to win;
> Go forth into the world's highway,
>     Compel the wanderer to come in.
>
> Toil on, and in thy toil rejoice;
>     For toil comes rest, for exile home;
> Soon shalt thou hear the Bridegroom's voice,
>     The midnight cry, 'Behold, I come!'

J.I. Packer

*Notes*
1. *Memoirs of Thomas Boston* (Banner of Truth, 1988), p.48.
2. p. 10.   3. *ibid*.   4. p. 11.

# Introduction

AH! Lord, who hath believed our report? and to whom is the arm of the Lord revealed? This day seems to be a day of darkness and gloominess; the glory is departed even to the threshold of the temple. We may call ordinances Ichabod; and name the faithful preachers of Scotland no more Naomi, but Mara, for the Lord deals bitterly with them, in so much forsaking his ordinances as at this day. The Lord hath forsaken them in a great measure, as to success attending their labours. They toil all the night; but little or nothing is caught; few or none can they find to come into the net. So that Jeremiah's exercise may be theirs, 'If ye will not hear it, my soul shall weep in secret places for your pride; and mine eye shall weep sore, and run down with tears' (13:17)

And thou, O my soul, mayst make this thy exercise, if thou hadst a heart that could mourn either for thyself or others. Though indeed it is no great wonder that God does not countenance with much success the like of me, who (if I may or dare class myself among those that are faithful) am the meanest, the most unworthy of them all, not worthy to take his covenant in my mouth, who am a child in piety and the mystery of godliness, though not in years; who am a poor fool, having a weak heart and a shallow head; who might rather be learning of others than teaching them; who can but wade about the outer parts of that depth, into which others can enter far; who have so little love to Christ, and so little pure zeal for his glory; can say so little for the truth, and so little against error; who am altogether unworthy and insufficient for these things; no wonder, I say, God does not countenance me, when others, that are as tall cedars in the Lord's vineyard, do so little good, even others that are great men in the church for piety and learning. But yet seeing I am called out to preach this everlasting gospel, it is my duty to endeavour, and it is my desire to be (Lord, thou knowest) a fisher of men.

But, alas! I may come in with my complaints to my Lord, that I have toiled in some measure, but caught nothing, for anything I know, as to the conversion of any one soul. I fear I may say, I have almost spent my strength in vain, and my labour for nought, for Israel is not gathered. O my soul, what may be the cause of this, why does my preaching so little good? No doubt part of the blame lies on myself, and a great part of it too.

But who can give help in this case but the Lord

himself? and how can I expect it from him but by prayer, and faith in the promises, and by consulting his word, where I may, by his Spirit shining on my heart, (shine, O Sun of righteousness), learn how to carry, and what to do, to the end the gospel preached by me may not be unsuccessful?

Therefore did my heart cry out after Christ this day, and my soul was moved, when I read that sweet promise of Christ: *Follow me, and I will make you fishers of men* (Matt. 4:19), directed to those that would follow him. O how fain would my soul follow him, as on other accounts, so on this, that I might be honoured to be a fisher of men; therefore my soul would fain know what sort of following Christ this is, to which this sweet promise is annexed. I would know it, (Lord, thou knowest), that I might do it, and so catch poor souls by the gospel, and that I might know whether I have a right to this promise or not.

O let thy light and thy truth shine forth, that they may be guides to me in this matter; and let the meditations of my heart be according to thy mind, and directed by thy unerring Spirit. Grant light and life, O Lord my God.

# PART ONE

# THE PROMISE AND THE DUTY

*Follow me, and I will make you fishers of men.* In these words there are two things to be considered.

## 1. There is a duty, *Follow me*

Wherein consider first the object, *me*, even the Lord Jesus Christ, the chief fisher of men, who was sent by the Father to gather in the lost sheep of the house of Israel, who was and is the infinitely-wise God, and so knew the best way to catch men, and can instruct men how to be fishers of others.

Next, consider the act, *Follow* (Gr. *come after*) *me*: Leave your employment, and come after me. Though no doubt there is a direction here to all the ministers of the gospel, that have left their other employments, and betaken themselves to the preaching of the word, viz., that if they would do good to souls, and gain them by their ministry, then they are to imitate Christ, in their carriage and preaching, to make him their pattern, to write after his copy, as a fit mean for gaining of souls.

## 2. There is a promise annexed to the duty

Wherein we may consider:

(a) The benefit promised; that is, to be *made fishers of men*; which I take to be not only an investing of them with authority, and a calling of them to the office, but also a promise of the success they should have, that fishing of men should be their employment, and they should not be employed in vain, but following Christ, they should indeed catch men by the gospel.

(b) The fountain-cause of this, *I, I will make you*; none other can make you fishers of men but me.

Thou mayest observe first then, O my soul, *that it is the Lord Jesus Christ that makes men fishers of men.* Here I shall shew:

(1) How Christ makes men fishers of men.

(2) Why unconverted men are compared to fish in the water.

(3) That ministers are fishers by office.

# 1

## HOW DOES CHRIST MAKE MEN FISHERS OF MEN?

In answer to this question, consider spiritual fishing two ways: first, as to the office and work itself; and second, as to the success of it.

*First*, he makes them fishers as to their office, by his call, which is twofold, outward and inward, by setting them apart to the office of the ministry; and it is thy business, O my soul, to know whether thou hast it or not. But of this more afterwards.

*Second*, he makes them fishers as to success; that is, he makes them catch men to himself by the power of his Spirit accompanying the word they preach, and the discipline they administer:

> The preaching of the cross - unto us which are saved, is the power of God (1 Cor. 1:18).

> Our gospel came not unto you in word only, but also in power, and in the Holy Ghost, and in much assurance (1 Thess. 1:5).

He it is that brings sinners into the net which ministers spread; and if he be not with them to drive the fish into the net, they may toil all the night, and day too, and catch nothing.

O my soul, then see that gifts will not do the business. A man may preach as an angel, and yet be useless. If Christ withdraw his presence, all will be to no purpose. If the Master of the house be away, the household will loath their food, though it be dropping down about their tent-doors.

Why shouldst thou then, on the one hand, as sometimes thou art, be lifted up when thou preachest a good and solid discourse, wherein gifts do appear, and thou gettest the applause of men? Why, thou mayst do all this, and yet be no fisher of men. The fish may see the bait, and play about it as pleasant, but this is not enough to catch them.

On the other hand, why shouldst thou be so much discouraged (as many times is the case), because thy gifts are so small, and thou art but as a child in com-parison of others? Why, if Christ will, he can make thee a fisher of men, as well as the most learned rabbi in the church: *Out of the mouths of babes and sucklings hast thou ordained strength* (Ps. 8:2). Yea, hast thou not observed how God owned a man very weak in gifts and made him more successful than others that were far beyond him in parts? Has not God put this treasure in earthen vessels, that the power might be seen to be of him? Lift up thyself then, O my soul, Christ can make thee a fisher of men, however weak thou art. Follow thou him. My soul desires to follow hard after thee, O God!

Be concerned then, in the first place, O my soul, for the presence of God in ordinances, and for his power that will make a change among people (Ps. 110:3). When thy discourse, though ever so elaborate, shall be but as a lovely song, O set thyself most for this. When thou studiest, send up ejaculations to thy Lord for it. When thou writest a sermon, or dost ruminate on it, then say to God, 'Lord, this will be altogether weak without thy power accompanying it.'

O power and life from God in ordinances is sweet. Seek it for thyself, and seek it for thy hearers. Acknowledge thine own weakness and uselessness without it, and so cry incessantly for it, that the Lord may drive the fish into the net, when thou art spreading it out. Have an eye to this power, when thou art preaching; and think not thou to convert men by the force of reason: if thou do, thou wilt be beguiled.

What an honourable thing is it to be fishers of men! How great an honour shouldst thou esteem it, to be a catcher of souls! *We are workers together with God*, says the apostle. If God has ever so honoured thee, O that thou knewest it that thou mightst bless his holy name, that ever made such a poor fool as thee to be a co-worker with him. God has owned thee to do good to those who were before caught. O my soul, bless thou the Lord. Lord, what am I, or what is my father's house, that thou hast brought me to this?

Then seest thou not here what is the reason thou toilest so long, and catchest nothing? The power comes not along. Men are like Samuel, who, when God was calling him, thought it had been Eli. So when thou speakest many times, they do not discern God's voice, but thine; and therefore the word goes out as it comes in.

Then, O my soul, despair not of the conversion of any, be they ever so profligate. For it is the power of the Spirit that drives any person into the net; and this cannot be resisted. Mockers of religion, yea, blasphemers may be brought into the net; and many times the wind of God's Spirit in the word lays the tall cedars in sin down upon the ground, when they that seem to be as low shrubs in respect of them, stand fast upon their root. Publicans and harlots shall enter the kingdom of heaven before self-righteous Pharisees.

What thinkest thou, O my soul, of that doctrine that lays aside this power of the Spirit, and makes moral suasion all that is requisite to the fishing of men? That doctrine is hateful to thee. My soul loaths it, as attributing too much to the preacher, and too much to corrupt nature in taking away its natural impotency to good, and as against the work of God's Spirit, contrary to experience; and is to me a sign of the rottenness of the heart that embraces it. Alas! that it should be owned by any among us, where so much of the Spirit's power has been felt.

## 2

## BUT WHY ARE UNCONVERTED MEN COMPARED TO FISH IN THE WATER?

Among other reasons, they are so because as the water is the natural element of fish, so sin is the proper and natural element for an unconverted soul. Take the fish out of the water, it cannot live; and take from a natural man his idols, he is ready to say with Micah, *Ye have taken away my gods, and what have I more*? The young man in the gospel could not be persuaded to seek after treasure in heaven, and lay by the world. It is in sin that the only delight of natural men is; but in holiness they have no more delight than a fish upon the earth, or a sow in a palace.

Oh, the woeful case of a natural man! Bless the Lord, O my soul, that when that was thy element as well as that of others, yet Christ took thee in his net, held thee, and would not let thee go, and put another principle in thee, so that now it is heavy for thee to wade, far more to swim in these waters.

The fish in a sunny day are seen to play themselves in the water. So the unregenerate, whatever grief they may seem to have upon their spirits, when a storm arises, either without, by outward troubles, or within by conscience-gnawing convictions, yet when these are over, and they are in a prosperous state, they play themselves in the way of sin, and take their pleasure in it, not considering what it may cost them at the last. Oh! how does prosperity in the world ruin many a soul! The prosperity of fools shall destroy them. And how destructive would prosperity have been to thee, O my soul, if God had given it to thee many times when thou wouldst have had it! Bless the Lord that ever he was pleased to cross thee in a sinful course.

As the fish greedily look after and snatch at the bait, not minding the hook; even so natural men drink in sin greedily, as the ox drinketh in the water. They look on sin as a sweet morsel; and it is to them sweet in the mouth, though bitter in the belly. They play with it, as the fish with the bait; but, Oh! alas, when they take the serpent in their bosom, they mind not the sting (Prov. 9:17, 18). The devil knows well how to dress his hooks; but, alas! men know not by nature how to discern them.

Pity then, O my soul, the wicked of the world, whom thou seest greedily satisfying their lusts. Alas! they are poor blinded souls; they see the bait, but not the hook; and therefore it is that they are even seen as it were dancing about the mouth of the pit; therefore rush they on to sin as a horse to the battle, not knowing the hazard. O pity the poor drunkard, the swearer, the unclean person, etc., that is wallowing in his sin.

Bless thou the Lord also, O my soul, that when thou wast playing with the bait, and as little minding the hook as others, God opened thine eyes, and let thee see thy madness and danger, that thou mightst flee from it. And be now careful that thou snatch at none of the devil's baits, lest he catch thee with his hook, for though thou mayst be restored again by grace, yet it shall not be without a wound; as the fish sometimes slip the hook, but go away wounded; which wound may be sad to thee, and long a-healing. And this thou hast experienced.

As fish in the water love deep places and wells, and are most frequently found there, so wicked men have a great love to carnal security, and have no will to strive against the stream. Fish love deep places best, where there is least noise. Oh, how careful are natural men to keep all quiet, that there may be nothing to disturb them in their rest in sin! They love to be secure, which is their destruction. O my soul, beware of carnal security, of being secure, though plunged over head and ears in sin.

As fish are altogether unprofitable as long as they are in the water, so are wicked men in their natural estate, they can do nothing that is really good: they are unprofitable to themselves, and unprofitable to others: what good they do to others, is more *per accidens* than *per se* (Rom. 3:12).

How far must they then be mistaken, who think the wicked of the world the most useful in the place where they live! They may indeed be useful for carrying on designs for Satan's interest, or their own vain glory; but really to lay out themselves for God, they cannot.

## 3

# MINISTERS ARE FISHERS
# BY OFFICE

They are catchers of the souls of men, sent 'to open the eyes of the blind, and to turn them from darkness to light, and from the power of Satan unto God'. Preachers of the gospel are fishers, and their work and that of fishers agree in several things.

The design and work of fishers is to catch fish. This is the work that preachers of the gospel have taken in hand, even to endeavour to bring souls to Christ. Their design in their work should be the same.

Tell me, O my soul, what is thy design in preaching? For what end dost thou lay the net in the water? Is it to show thy gifts, and to gain the applause of men? Oh, no! Lord, thou knowest my gifts are very small; and had I not some other thing than them to lean to, I had never gone to a pulpit. I confess that, for as small as they are, the devil and my corruptions do sometimes present them to me in a magnifying glass, and so would blow me up with wind. But, Lord, thou knowest it is my work to repel these motions. An instance of this see in my Diary.[1]

Their work is hard work; they are exposed to much cold in the water. So is the minister's work.

A storm that will affright others, they will venture on, that they may not lose their fish. So should preachers of the gospel do.

Fishers catch fish with a net. So preachers have a net to catch souls with. This is the everlasting gospel, the word of peace and reconciliation, wherewith sinners are caught.

It is compared to a net wherewith fishers catch fish, first, because it is spread out, ready to catch all that will come into it:

Ho, every one that thirsteth, come ye to the waters; and he that hath no money, come ye, buy and eat; yea, come buy wine and milk, without money, and without price (Isa. 55:1).

---

1. January 1, 1699. I had more than an ordinary measure of God's presence and help in preaching. In the morning in Secret I was earnest with God for it, but had a temptation to think that God would leave me, which did perplex me sore. When I was coming home from the Sermons, Satan fell to, afresh again, the contrary way, tempting me to pride. It came three times remarkably on me, and was as often repelled by that word, 'What hast thou that thou has not received?'

God excludes none from the benefits of the gospel that will not exclude themselves; it is free to all.

Second, because as fish are taken unexpectedly by the net, so are sinners by the gospel. Zaccheus was little thinking on salvation from Christ when he went to the tree. Paul was not thinking on a sweet meeting with Christ, whom he persecuted, when he was going post-haste on the devil's errand; but the man is caught unexpectedly. Little wast thou thinking, O my soul, on Christ, heaven or thyself, when thou went to the Newton of Whitsome to hear a preaching, when Christ first dealt with thee; there thou got an unexpected cast.

Third, as fish sometimes come near and touch the net, and yet draw back; so many souls are somewhat affected at the hearing of the gospel, and yet remain in the gall of bitterness and the bond of iniquity. So Herod heard John the Baptist gladly, but yet the poor man was not caught. Wonder not then, O my soul, that thou seest some affected in the time of preaching; and yet when they are away again, all is worn off.

Fourth, some fish that have not been taken fast hold enough by the net, struggle, and get out again. So some souls have their convictions, and may seem to be caught; but yet, alas! they stifle all their convictions, stay in the place of the breaking forth; their goodness is like the morning cloud, and as the early dew that soon passeth away. Wherefore, O my soul, if ever thou be taken up with exercised consciences, have a care that thou do not apply the cure before the wound be deep enough. Take all means to understand whether the soul be content to take Christ on his own terms or not. Alas! many this way, by having the wound scurfed over, are rather killed than cured.

Fifth, all that are taken in the net do make some struggling to get free. Even so every one whom the Lord deals with by his word and Spirit, make some kind of resistance before they are thoroughly caught. *Cras, Domine*, says Augustine; *et modo, Domine, donec, modo non haberet modum*. And this thou also knowest, O my soul, how thou wouldst have been content to have been out of the net. Oh! the wickedness of the heart of man by nature! opposite is it, and an enemy to all that may be for its eternal welfare. There is indeed a power in our will to resist, yea, and such a power as cannot but be exercised by the will of man, which can do nothing but resist, till the overcoming power of God, the *gratia victrix*, come and make the unwilling heart willing (Phil. 2:13).

Sixth, yet this struggling will not do with those which the net has fast enough. So neither will the resistance do that is made by an elect soul, whom God intends to catch: *All that the Father hath given me, shall come to me* (John 6:37). Indeed, God does not convert men to himself against their will, he does not force the soul to receive Christ; but he conquers the will, and it becomes obedient. He that was unwilling before, is then willing. O the power of grace! When God speaks, then men shall hear; then is it that the dead hear the voice of the Son of Man, and they that hear do live.

Seventh, in a net are many meshes in which the fish are caught. Such are the invitations made to sinners in the gospel, the sweet promises made to them that will come to Christ; these are the meshes wherewith the soul is catched. This then is gospel-preaching, thus to spread out the net of the gospel, wherein are so many meshes of various invitations and promises, to which if the fish do come, they are caught.

Eighth, lest the net be lifted up with the water, and so not fit for taking fish, and the fish slight it and pass under it; there are some pieces of lead put to it to hold it right in the water that it may be before them as they come. So lest invitations and promises of the gospel be slighted, there must be used some legal terrors and law-threatenings to drive the fish into the net. Thou seest then that both law and gospel are to be preached, the law as a pendicle of the gospel-net, which makes it effectual; the law being a schoolmaster to bring us to Christ.

Ninth, the meshes must not be over-wide, lest the fish run through. So neither must thy doctrine be general, without particular application, lest thou be no fisher of men. Indeed men may be the better pleased, when thou preachest doctrine so as wicked men may run out-through and in-through it, than when thou makest it so as to take hold of them; but be not a servant of men.

Tenth, neither must they be too neat and fine, and curiously wrought, lest they hold out the fish. So have a care, O my soul, of striving to make by wit any fine and curious discourse, which thy hearers cannot understand. Of this more afterwards.

Fishers observe in what places they should cast their nets, and where they may expect fish. So do thou, O my soul, observe where thou mayst catch souls.

There are two pools wherein the net should be set; in the public assemblies of the Lord's people. There it was that Lydia's heart was opened. The pool of ordinances sometimes is made healing water to souls pining away in their iniquity. The second place to set a net is in private conference. Many times the Lord is pleased to bless this for the good of souls. Some have found it so. But more of these things afterwards, when I come to following Christ.

Fishers may toil long, and yet catch nothing; but they do not therefore lay aside their work. So may preachers preach long, and yet not catch any soul (Isa. 49:4, and 53:1) but they are not to give up for all that.

O my soul, here thou art checked for thy behaviour at some times under the absence of Christ from ordinances, when thou hast been ready to wish thou hadst never taken it in hand. This was my sin: the good Lord pardon it. It becomes me better to lie low under God's hand, and to inquire into the causes of his withdrawing his presence from me and from ordinances, and yet to hold on in duty till he be pleased to lay me by. Have a care of that, O my soul, and let not such thoughts and wishes possess thee again. Forget not how God made thee to read this thy sin, in thy punishment (Diary, November 13, 1698).

Hold on, O my soul, and give not way to these discouragements. Thou knowest not but Christ may come and teach thee to let down the net at the right side of the ship, and thou mayst yet be a fisher of men. Trust God thou shalt yet praise him for the help of his countenance as thou hast done, and perhaps for some souls that thou mayst be yet honoured to catch.

# PART TWO

# HOW MAY I COME BY THIS ART?

And thus I have briefly considered these things. But the main question that I would have resolved is, How may I come by this art? What way I shall take to be a fisher of men? How I may order and set the net, that it may bring in souls to God? This the great Master of assemblies sets down in the first part of the verse.

Observe, O my soul, that the way for me to be a fisher of men, is to follow Christ. What it is to follow thee, O Lord, shew me; and, Lord, help me to do it.

Here two things are to be considered:

(1) What following Christ supposes and implies.

(2) Wherein Christ is to be followed.

# 1

## WHAT FOLLOWING CHRIST
## SUPPOSES AND IMPLIES

### 1. It presupposes life

A dead man cannot follow any person; a dead preacher cannot follow Christ; there must be a principle of life, spiritual life in him, or else he is nought. Therefore have I said and maintained, that a man cannot be a minister *in foro Dei*, though he may *in foro ecclesiae*, without grace in his heart. This is a spiritual following of Christ; and therefore presupposes a spiritual and heavenly principle.

Tell me then, O my soul, what state art thou in? Thou wast once dead, that is sure, *dead in trespasses and sins* (Eph. 2:1). Art thou raised out of thy grave? Hast thou got a part in the first resurrection? Has Christ breathed on thy dead and dry bones? Or art thou yet void of spiritual life? Art thou rotting away in thine iniquity? What sayest thou to this? If thou be yet dead, thy case is lamentable; but if thou be alive, what signs of life are there to be seen in thee?

I have my own doubts of this, because of the

prevailing of corruption: therefore I will see what I can say to this.

A man that hath the Spirit hath life (Rom. 8: 2, 9) but I think I have the Spirit: *ergo*, I have life. That I have the Spirit, I conclude from these grounds following.

## 1. I have light that sometimes I had not

> The Comforter ... shall teach you all things, and bring all things to your remembrance, whatsoever I have said unto you (John 14:26).

I see now otherwise than sometimes I saw. Once was I blind, but now I see, though I see but men as trees. Once was I darkness, but now am I light (though weak) in the Lord. This light makes me see:

(a) My former darkness, the sad and miserable state that once I was in, ignorant of God, Christ, and religion, save going to the church, and keeping from banning and swearing, etc., which I was restrained from, from a child. This makes me see my present darkness (1 Cor. 13:12). How little a portion do I know of thee, O God? My knowledge is but as the twilight.

(b) It lets me see my heart sins, my imperfections and shortcomings in the best of my duties;

so that God might damn me for them. The hypocrites say, *Why have we fasted, and thou seest not?* (Isa. 58:3). It lets me see the wanderings of my heart in duty and out of duty, yea, the sinfulness of the first risings of lust in mine heart (Rom. 7), and is still discovering the baseness of my heart unto me, so that I am forced to think and say that at the best I am unclean, unclean.

(c) It makes me to see Christ precious (1 Pet. 2:7), altogether lovely, the chief among ten thousand, preferable to all the world; for whom if my heart deceive me not (Lord, thou knowest), I would undergo the loss of that which I most esteem in the world. 'Whom have I in heaven but thee? and there is none on earth that I desire besides thee.' For indeed, 'My heart and flesh faints and fails; but thou art the strength of my heart, O LORD' (Ps. 73:25, 26).

(d) It lets me see my need of him; so that nothing else but Christ, I am persuaded, can help me. When I have done what I can, I am but an unprofitable servant. If I should do a thousand times more than I do, I count all but loss and dung for the excellency of the knowledge of Jesus Christ my Lord. My soul cries out for thee, O God, and follows hard after thee.

(e) The knowledge that I have of Christ makes me trust in him in some measure (Ps. 9:10), though alas! my evil heart of unbelief creates a great deal of difficulty in that to me. I find him a present help in the time of trouble; therefore I endeavour to cast my burden upon him. I know him to be a good Master, and therefore I lean on him for help for his own work. I know his grace is sufficient for me; therefore in temptation and trials, I endeavour to lift up my soul to him.

## 2. I feel help in duty from the Spirit

I know not what I should pray for; but the Spirit helpeth my infirmities (Rom. 8:26). Many times I have gone to prayer very dead, and have come away with life; I have gone with a drooping and fainting heart, and come away rejoicing; with an heart closed, and have come away with an heart enlarged, and have felt enlargement both as to words and affections; and this hath made me both thankful and more vile in mine own eyes, that God should have done so with the like of me (1 Chr. 29:14).

He that hath sense and feeling hath life; but I have sense and feeling; *ergo*, I have life (Eph. 4:19). My sins are a burden to me (Matt. 11:28). Lord, thou knowest my omissions and commissions, the sins of my thoughts and of my life, the sins of my youth, and above all, that which is my daily trouble, an evil, backsliding and base heart, which I find deceitful above all things and desperately wicked (Jer. 17:9). This body of sin and death makes me to groan, and long to be rid of it (Rom. 7:24). And what a load it was to me this day, God knows. I feel God's presence, which makes me to rejoice sometimes; at other times again I feel his absence. Thou, O Lord, hidest thy face, and I am troubled (Ps. 30:7). His smiles are sweet as honey from the comb, and his frowns are bitter as death to my soul.

He in whom there is heat hath life; but I have a heat in my soul; *ergo*, I have life. I find a threefold flame, though weak, in my heart.

## 1. *A flame of love to Christ (Rom. 5:5)*

My soul loves him above all; and I have felt my love to Christ more vigorous within this short while than for a considerable time before. Lord, put fuel to this flame.

I have a love to his truths that I know, what God reveals to me of his word (Ps. 119:19). I find sometimes his word sweeter to me than honey from the comb (Ps. 19:10). It comforts and supports me. I cannot but love it; it stirs me up, and quickens my soul when dead.

I love his commands, though striking against my corruptions (Rom. 7:22).

I love the promises, as sweet cordials to a fainting soul, as life from the dead to one trodden under foot by the apprehensions of wrath, or the prevailing of corruption.

I love his threatenings as most just; my soul heartily approves them. *If any man love not the Lord Jesus, let him be anathema, maranatha.* The least part of truth, that God makes known to me, I love; and, by grace, would endeavour to adhere to.

I love those in whom the image of God does appear; though otherwise mean and contemptible, my heart warms towards them (1 John 3:14).

I love his work, and am glad when it thrives (Rom. 1:8), though alas! there is little ground for such gladness now.

I love his ordinances (Ps. 84:1) and what bears his stamp; though all this be but weak, I love his glory, that he should be glorified, come of me what will.

*2. I find in my heart a flame of desires after the righteousness of Christ (Matt. 5:6)*

My soul earnestly desires to be stript naked of my own righteousness, which is as rags, and to be clothed and adorned with the robe of his righteousness. This wedding garment my soul affects; so shall I be found without spot, when the Master of the feast comes in to see the guests. My soul is satisfied, and acquiesces in justification by an imputed righteousness, though, alas! my base heart would fain have a home-spun garment of its own sometimes.

I also find in my heart a flame of desires after communion with him (Ps. 42:1). When I want it my soul though sometimes careless, yet, at other times, cries out, *O that I knew where I might find him!* I have found much sweetness in communion with God, especially at the sacrament of the Lord's Supper, in prayer and meditation, hearing the word faithfully and seriously preached, and in preaching it myself, when the candle of the Lord shines on my tabernacle; then was it a sweet exercise to my soul.

I endeavour to keep it up when I have it, by watching over my heart and sending up ejaculations to God. When I want it, I cry to him for it, though, alas! I have been a long time very careless. Sometimes my soul longs for the day, when my minority shall be over-past and I be entered heir to *the inheritance incorruptible, undefiled, and that fadeth not away;* to be quit of this evil world; to be dissolved, and to be with Christ, which is best of all; especially at three times.

(a) When I get more than ordinarily near God,

when my soul is satisfied as with marrow and fat, when my heart is nobilitated, and tramples on the world.

(b) When I am wrestling and groaning under the body of sin and death, the evil heart: then fain would I be there, where Satan cannot tempt, and sin cannot enter; yea, when I have been much forsaken, at least as to comfort (Diary, August 2, 1696, where is the most eminent instance of it).

(c) When I preach, and see that the gospel hath not success, but people are unconcerned, and go on in their abominations.

### 3. I find in my heart some heat of zeal for God, which vents itself first, by endeavouring to be active for God in my station

So when I was at K. I endeavoured to do something for God, though, alas! it did some of them no good. Before I entered on trials, one main motive was to have opportunity to give a testimony against sin, and to see if I could be an instrument to reclaim any soul from their wicked way. This I have, as the Lord enabled me, done since I was a preacher, testifying against sin freely and plainly, and as earnestly as I could, by grace assisting me, though in weakness. And, Lord, thou knowest that my great desire is to catch men, and to get for that end my whole furniture from thee, laying aside my own wisdom. And if I could do this, how satisfying would it be to my soul, that desires to do good to others, though I myself should perish?

Therefore do I not spare this weak body, and therefore have I desired never to be idle, but to go unsent for sometimes. Yet my conscience tells me of much slackness in this point, when I have been in private with people and have not reproved them as I ought when they offended, being much plagued with want of freedom in private converse. This I have in the Lord's strength resolved against, and have somewhat now amended it.

Second, it vents itself in indignation against sin in myself and others. Many times have I thought on that of the apostle, *Yea, what revenge!* when I have been overcome by a temptation, being content as it were to be revenged on myself, and as it were content to subscribe a sentence of damnation against myself, and so to justify the Lord in his just proceedings against me. And, *Lord, do not I hate those that hate thee! am I not grieved with those that rise up against thee? The reproaches cast on thee, have fallen on me* (Ps. 69:9). And my heart rises and is grieved when I see transgressors, that they keep not thy law.

Third, it vents itself in grieving for those

things that I cannot help. Lord, thou knowest
how weighty the sins of this land have been unto
me, how they have lien and do lie somewhat
heavy on me; and at this time in particular, the
laxness of many in joining with the people of
these abominations, the unfaithfulness of some
professors, the lack of zeal for God in not making
a more narrow search for the accursed thing in
our camp, now when God's wrath is going out
violently against us, and not making an acknowl-
edgement of sins and renewing our national
vows, according as our progenitors did, many as
it were thinking shame of the covenant, of whom
the Church of Scotland may be ashamed.

Growth and motion is an evidence of life (Ps.
92:12-14). I move forward toward heaven, my
affections are going out after Christ, and endeav-
ouring to make progress in a Christian walk. I
think I discern a growth of these graces in me.

(1) A growth of knowledge and acquaintance
with Christ (2 Pet. 3:18). I am more acquainted
with Christ and his ways than before. Though I
have not such uptakings of Christ as I ought to
have, yet I have more than I have had in this
respect sometimes before.

(2) A growth of love. If my heart deceive me
not, I have found love to Christ within this month

more lively and vigorous than before, my soul more affected with his absence from ordinances than ever.

(3) A growth of faith. I can, I think, trust God more now than before. I have had more experience of his goodness and knowledge of his name; and therefore think I can cast my burden on the Lord better than before. But it is easy swimming when the head is held up. Lord, increase my faith. I believe, Lord, help mine unbelief.

(4) A growth of watchfulness. I have felt the sad effects of unwatchfulness over my heart in times past. I feel the good of watchfulness now; my soul is habitually more watchful than before; neither dare I give such liberty to my heart as sometimes I gave. Yet for all this the Lord may well complain of me, that he is broken with my wanton heart. But, Lord, thou knowest it is also breaking to myself that it is so. The Lord seal these things to me.

(5) A growth of contempt of the world, which, blessed be God, is on the increase with me.

## 2. Following Christ implies a knowledge of the way that Christ took

No man can follow the example of another as such, unless he know what way he lived. So neither can any man follow Christ with respect to the catching of men in particular, unless he know Christ's way of catching souls, that is, so far as it may be followed by us. Acquaint then thyself, O my soul, with the history of the gospel wherein this appears, and take special notice of these things, that thou mayest follow Christ. What a sad case must they be in that are not acquainted with this!

## 3. Following Christ supposes sense of weakness, and the need of a guide

A man that knows a way and can do well enough without a guide, needs not follow another. And surely the want of this is the reason why many run before Christ, and go farther than his example ever called them; and others take a way altogether different from Christ's way, which is the product of their own conceited hearts and airy heads. But thou, O my soul, acknowledge thyself as a child in these matters, that cannot go unless it be led; as a stranger in a desert place that cannot keep the right way without a guide. Acknowledge and be affected with thine own weakness and emptiness, which thou mayst well be persuaded of. And of this end reflect seriously:

(1) On that word: *Who is sufficient for these things?* (2 Cor. 2:16). No man is of himself sufficient; even the greatest of men come short of

sufficiency. This may make thee then to be affected with insufficiency, who are so far below these men, as shrubs are below the tall cedars; and yet they cannot teach it of themselves.

(2) Consider the weight of the work, even of preaching, which is all that thou hast to do now. It is the concern of souls. By the foolishness of preaching it pleases the Lord to save them that believe; and as thou thoughtest yesterday (January 22, 1699) before thou went to the pulpit, it may seal the salvation of some, and the damnation of others. To preach in the Spirit, in the power and demonstration thereof, is no easy matter. Thy pitiful gifts will not fit thee for this.

(3) Reflect on what thou art when God is pleased to desert thee: how then thou tuggest and rowest, but it will not do, either in studying or delivering sermons. I think thou hast had as much of this as may teach thee to beware of taking thy burden on thy own soul, but to cast it on the Lord. (See Diary, June 3, July 3, December 31, 1698; January 6, 1699, etc.)

(4) Consider what a small portion thou knowest of God. When thou art at the best, and when thou art in thy meridian, yet how low art thou? And how far short thou comest of what thou shouldst be at.

(5) Consider that though thou hadst gifts like

an angel, yet thou canst not convert a soul unless Christ be with thee to do the work. Therefore acknowledge thyself a weak creature, insufficient for the work; and go not out in thy own strength, but in the name of the Lord; and so although thou be but as a stripling, thou mayst be helped to cast down the great Goliaths that defy the armies of the living God.

## 4. Following Christ implies a renouncing of our own wisdom

It must not be the guide that we must follow (Matt. 16:24). Paul would not preach with wisdom of words (1 Cor. 1:17), he did not follow the rules of carnal wisdom.

Therefore, O my soul, renounce thine own wisdom. Seek the wisdom that is from above; seek to preach the words of the living God, and not thine own. Since thou wast most set to take this way, and prayed most that thou mightst not preach that which might be the product of thy own wisdom and natural reason, but that which might be given thee of the Holy Ghost, thou hast found that God hath signally countenanced thee.

Take not the way of natural wisdom, follow not the rules of carnal wisdom. Its language will always be, *Master, spare thyself*; have a care of thy credit and reputation among men. If thou speak freely, they will call thee a railer, and thy preaching reflections; every parish will scare at thee as a monster of men, and one that would preach them all to hell; and so thou shalt not be settled. Such and such a man, that has a great influence in a parish, will never like thee. That way of preaching is not the way to gain people; that startles them at the very first. You may bring them on by little and little, by being somewhat smooth, at least at the first: for this generation is not able to abide such doctrine as that thou preachest.

But hear thou and follow the rules of the wisdom that is from above: for the wisdom of the world is foolishness with God; that which is in high esteem among men, is nought in the sight of God. The wisdom that is from above will tell thee, that thou must be denied to thy credit and reputation, etc. (Matt. 16:24; Luke 14:26). It will tell thee, Let them call thee what they will, that thou must *cry aloud, and spare not; lift up thy voice like a trumpet* etc. (Isa. 58:1). It will tell thee that *God has appointed the bounds of men's habitation* (Acts 17:26). It will tell thee that *not many wise, not many mighty, not many noble, are called* (1 Cor. 1:26). *Whether they will hear, or whether they will forbear, thou shalt speak God's words unto them* (Ezek. 2:7). It will shew thee

63

rules quite contrary to those of carnal wisdom. Let me consider then what carnal wisdom says to me, and what the wisdom from above says.

| CARNAL WISDOM | SPIRITUAL WISDOM |
|---|---|
| Thy body is weak, spare it, and weary it not; it cannot abide toil, labour, and weariness; spare thyself then. | Your body is God's as well as your spirit; spare it not for glorifying God (1 Cor. 6:20). 'In weariness and painfulness' (2 Cor. 11:27). 'He giveth power to the faint, and to them that have no might he increaseth strength' (Isa. 40:29). This thou hast experienced. |
| Labour to get neat and fine expressions; for these do very much commend a preaching to the learned; and without these they think nothing of it. | Christ sent thee to 'preach the gospel not with wisdom of words' (1 Cor. 1:17). Go not to them with 'excellency of speech, or of wisdom' (1 Cor. 2:1). Let not thy speech and preaching be with 'the enticing words of man's wisdom' (verse 4). |
| Endeavour to be somewhat smooth in preaching, and calm; and do not | 'Cry aloud, and spare not, lift up thy voice like a trumpet: shew my people |

go out upon the particular sins of the land, or of the persons to whom thou preachest.

If thou wilt not do so, they will be irritated against thee, and may create thee trouble; and what a foolish thing would it be for thee to speak boldly to such a generation as this, whose very looks are terrible!

It is a dangerous way to speak freely, and condescend on particulars; there may be more hazard in it than thou art aware of.

Thou wilt be looked on as a fool, as a monster of men; thou wilt be

their sins' (Isa. 58:1). 'Open rebuke is better than secret love' (Prov. 27:5). 'Study to shew thyself approved unto God, rightly dividing the word of truth' (2 Tim. 2:15).

'He that rebuketh a man, afterwards shall find more favour than he that flattereth with the tongue' (Prov. 28:23). I have experience of this. 'Fear them not, neither be afraid at their looks, though they be a rebellious house. I have made thy face strong against their faces' (Ezek. 3:8, 9). Experience confirms this.

'He that walketh uprightly, walketh surely' (Prov. 10:9). 'Whoso walketh uprightly shall be saved' (28:18).

'Thou must become a fool, that thou mayest be wise' (1 Cor. 3:18). 'We are

65

called a railer, and so lose thy reputation and credit, and thou hadst need to preserve that. Men will hate and abhor thee; and why shouldst thou expose thyself to these things?

made a spectacle to the world' (1 Cor. 4:9, 10). 'The servant is not greater than his lord,' (John 15:20, compared with 10:20), 'He hath a devil, and is mad, why hear ye him?' If thou wilt be Christ's disciple, 'thou must deny thyself' (Matt. 16:24). 'If the world hate you, ye know it hated me before it hated you,' (John 15:18) says our Lord.

Great people especially will be offended at you, if you speak not fair to them and court and caress them. And if you be looked down upon by great people, who are wise and mighty, what will you think of your preaching?

'Accept no man's person, neither give flattering titles to man: for, in so doing, thy Maker will soon take thee away' (Job 32:21, 22). 'Few of the rulers believe on Christ' (John 7:48). 'Not many wise men after the flesh, not many mighty, not many noble are called' (1 Cor. 1:26). 'Speak thou God's word to kings, and be not ashamed' (Ps. 119:46).

Our people are new come out from under Prelacy, and they would not desire to have sins told particularly, and especially old sores to be ripped up. They cannot abide that doctrine. Other doctrine would take better with them. Hold off such things; for it may well do them ill. It will do them no good.

'Thou shalt speak my words unto them, whether they will hear, or whether they will forbear, for they are most rebellious' (Ezek. 2:7). 'Give them warning from me. If thou do it not they shall die in their sins, but their blood will I require at thy hand' (3:17, 18). 'What the Lord saith to thee, that do thou speak' (1 Kings 22:14).

If you will preach such things, yet prudence requires that you speak of them very warily. Though conscience says you must, yet speak them somewhat covertly, that you may not offend them sore, and especially with respect to them that are but coming in yet, and do not fill them with prejudices at first; you may get occasion afterwards.

'Cry aloud, and spare not' (Isa. 58:1). 'Cursed be he that doth the work of the Lord deceitfully' (Jer. 48:10). 'Handle not the word of the Lord deceitfully.' Peter, at the first, told the Jews that were but coming in to hear, 'Him (Christ) ye have taken, and by wicked hands have crucified and slain' (Acts 2:23). 'Work while it is called today; the night cometh wherein thou canst not work' (John 9:4).

Be but fair especially to them that have the stroke in parishes, till you be settled in a parish to get stipend. If you will not do so, you may look for toiling up and down then; for parishes will scare at you, and will not call you, and how will you live? And so such a way of preaching will be to your loss, whereas otherwise it might be better with you.

'To have respect of persons is not good; for, for a piece of bread that man will transgress' (Prov. 28:21). 'The will of the Lord be done' (Acts 21:14). 'God hath determined your time, before appointed, and the bounds of your habitation' (Acts 17:26). 'And his counsel shall stand, oppose it who will' (Isa. 46:10). 'It is God that sets the solitary in families' (Ps. 68:6). 'If thou be faithful, thou shalt abound with blessings; but if thou makest haste to be rich, thou shalt not be innocent'

Thus thou seest, O my soul, how that carnal wisdom, notwithstanding it speaks fair and with a good deal of seeming reason, is quite contrary to the wisdom that is from above. It promiseth fair, but its promises are not always performed; it threatens sore, but neither do its threatenings always come to pass: it makes molehills mountains, and mountains molehills: therefore reject the wisdom of the world, for it is foolishness with God. Carnal policy would make thee fear him that can but kill the body, yea that cannot do so much now, and to cast off the true fear of God.

O my soul, remember that word, and make use of it for strengthening thee: *The fear of man bringeth a snare; but whoso putteth his trust in the Lord shall be safe* (Prov. 29:25). Never go to seek temporal profit by putting thy soul in hazard, but *wait* thou *on the Lord, and keep his way, and he shall exalt thee to inherit the land* (Ps. 37:34); for his way is the safest way, however carnal wisdom may speak otherwise of it and may account the following of it mere folly; but remember thou, that *the foolishness of God is wiser than men* (1 Cor. 1:25).

**5. Following Christ supposes, that we must not make men our rule, to follow them any farther than they follow Christ**

*Be ye followers of me,* says the apostle, *as I am of Christ* (1 Cor. 11:1). Wherein they follow Christ I may follow them, but in nothing else. All men are fallible; the greatest of men have had their own spots. Luther's opinion of Christ's corporal presence in the sacrament affords a notable instance of this.

Therefore, O my soul, let not man's authority prevail with thee to go off the road at all. If Christ himself tell thee not, O my soul, where he feedeth, thou mayst be left to turn aside to the flocks of his companions. Have a care of putting the servants of the Lord in his own room: but follow thou him.

## 2

# WHEREIN IS CHRIST
# TO BE FOLLOWED?

What are those things in him that I must imitate him in? What was the copy that he did cast, which I must write after, in order to my being a fisher of men? What he did by divine power is inimitable; I am not called to follow him in converting sinners by my own power; to work miracles for the confirmation of the doctrine that I preach, etc. But there are some things wherein he is imitable, and must be followed by preachers, if they would expect to be made fishers of men.

*First, Christ took not on him the work of preaching the gospel without a call*: 'For (says he) the Spirit of the Lord God is upon me, because the Lord hath anointed me to preach good tidings unto the meek, he hath sent me to bind up the broken-hearted, to proclaim liberty to the captives, and the opening of the prison to them that are bound' (Isa. 61:1). In this he must be followed by those that would be catchers of men. He was sent by the Father to preach the gospel; he went not to the work without his Father's commission. Men

71

must have a call to this work (Heb. 5:4). They that run unsent, that take on the work without a call from God, cannot expect to do good to a people (Rom. 10:14; Jer. 23). *I sent them not, therefore they shall not profit this people.* Tell me then, O my soul, whether thou hast thus followed Christ or not? Hadst thou a call from God to this work of the preaching of the gospel? Or hast thou run unsent?

In answer to this, I must consider that there is a twofold call, an extraordinary and an ordinary call. The first of these I was not to seek, nor may I pretend to it. The question then is, Whether I had an ordinary call from God or not to preach the gospel?

There are these four things in an ordinary call which do make it up.

(1) Knowledge of the doctrine of the Christian religion above that of ordinary professors (2 Tim. 3:16, 17). This I endeavoured to get by study, and prayer unto the Lord; and did attain to it in some measure, though far below the pitch that I would be at. My knowledge was lawfully tried by the church, and they were satisfied.

(2) Aptness to teach, some dexterity of communicating unto others that knowledge (1 Tim. 3:2; 2 Tim. 2:2). This was also tried by the church, and they were satisfied. This hath been

acknowledged by others whom I have taught; and God has given me some measure of it, however small.

(3) A will some way ready to take on the work of preaching the gospel (1 Pet. 5:2). This I had, for anything I know, since ever the Lord dealt with my soul, unless it was in a time of distress. And though I did a long time sit the call of the church, in not entering on trials, when they would have had me, yet this was not for want of will but ability for the work, and want of clearness for entering on such a great work at that time.

I had notwithstanding some desire to that work, which desire my conscience bears me witness, did not arise from the desire of worldly gain; for I would have desired that then, and would go on in the work now, though there were no such thing to be had by it, yea through grace, though I should meet with trouble for it.

Neither was it the love of vain glory, Lord, thou knowest, but that I might be capable to do something for God. I remember, that when I was a boy at the school, I desired to be a preacher of the gospel, because of all men ministers were most taken up about spiritual things. This my desire to the work did then run upon.

(4) The call of the church, which I had without

any motion from myself, not only to enter on trials, but, being approved, to preach the gospel as a probationer for the ministry; which does say, that what I have done in this work, I have not done without a call from God in an ordinary way, and that I have not run unsent. For confirmation of this my call, I refer to my Diary, some things to this purpose being noted there, all which I cannot here set down. Perhaps, if leisure permit, I shall extract them by themselves in order. Blessed be the Lord that made my darkness as noon day.

*Second, Christ designed his Father's glory in the work*. It was not honour, applause, and credit from men that he sought, but purely the Father's glory. Men that design not this, cannot be useful to the church, if it be not *per accidens*. This all actions are to level at; it is that which in all things should be designed as the ultimate end. *Whether therefore ye eat or drink, or whatsoever ye do, do all to the glory of God.*

Thou seest then that thou, O my soul, must follow Christ in this, if thou wouldst be a fisher of men. Lift up thy heart to this noble end, and in all, especially in thy preaching of the gospel, keep this before thine eyes. Beware of seeking thy own glory by preaching. Look not after popular applause; if thou do, thou hast thy reward (Matt. 6:2), look for no more.

O my soul, invert not the order: 'Thou, O Solomon, must have a thousand, and those that keep the fruit thereof two hundred' (Cant. 8:12). Have a care of taking a thousand to thyself, and giving God only two hundred. Let his honour be before thine eyes; trample on thy own credit and reputation, and sacrifice it, if need be, to God's honour. And to help thee to this, consider:

(1) That all thou hast is given thee of God. What hast thou that thou hast not received? What an unreasonable thing is it then not to use for his glory what he gives thee; yea, what ingratitude is it? And dost thou not hate the character of an ungrateful person? *Ingratum si dixeris, omnia dixeris.*

(2) Consider that what thou hast is a talent given thee by thy great Master to improve till he comes again. If thou improve it for him, then thou shalt get thy reward. If thou wilt make thy own gain thereby, and what thou shouldst improve for him, thou improve for thyself, what canst thou look for then but that God shall take thy talent from thee, and command to cast thee as an unprofitable and unfaithful servant into utter darkness, where shall be weeping and gnashing of teeth?

God has given some great talents; if they improve them for vain-glory to themselves to gain the popular applause, or the Hosannas of the learned, and so sacrifice all to their own net; what a sad meeting will such have at the great day with Christ? What master would endure that servant, to whom he has given money wherewith to buy a suit of good clothes to his master, if he should take that money, and buy therewith a suit to himself, which his master should have had? How can it be thought that God will suffer to go unpunished such a preacher as he has given a talent of gifts to, if he shall use these merely to gain a stipend or applause to himself therewith, not respecting the glory of his Master? Woe to thee, O my soul, if thou take this path wherein destroyers of men's souls and of their own go.

(3) Consider that the applause of the world is worth nothing. It is hard to be gotten; for readily the applause of the unlearned is given to him whom the learned despise, and the learned applaud him whom the common people care not for. And when it is got, what have you? A vain empty puff of wind. They think much of thee, thou thinkest much of thyself, and in the meantime God thinks nothing of thee. Remember, O my soul, what Christ said to the Pharisees: 'Ye are they which justify yourselves before men, but

God knoweth your hearts. For that which is highly esteemed among men, is an abomination in the sight of God' (Luke 16:15). Let this scare thee from seeking thyself.

(4) Consider, that seeking thy own glory is a dreadful and abominable thing.

First, in that thou then puttest thyself in God's room. His glory should be that which thou shouldst aim at, but then thy base self must be sacrificed too. O tremble at this, O my soul, and split not on this rock, otherwise thou shalt be dashed in pieces.

Second, in that it is the most gross dissembling with God that can be. Thou pretendest to preach Christ to a people; but seeking thy own glory, thou preachest thyself, and not him. Thou pretendest to be commending Christ and the ways of God to souls, and yet in the meantime thou commendest thyself. Will Christ sit with such a mocking of him? O my soul, beware of it; look not for it, but for his glory. Who would not take it for a base affront, to send a servant or a friend to court a woman for him, if he should court her for himself? And will not Christ be avenged on self-preaching ministers much more?

Third, in that it is base treachery and cruelty to the souls of hearers, when a man seeks to please their fancy more than to gain their souls, to get people to approve him more than to get them to approve themselves to God. This is a soul-murdering way, and it is dear-bought applause that is won by the blood of souls. O my soul, beware of this. Let them call thee what they will, but seek thou God's glory and their good.

(5) Consider that so to do is a shrewd sign of a graceless, Christless, and faithless heart: *How can ye believe, that receive honour one of another, and seek not the honour that cometh from God only?* (John 5:44). A grain of faith will cure this lightness of the head and heart.

(6) Consider, O my soul, thy own vileness. What art thou but a poor lump of clay, as to thy body, that will soon return to the dust, and be a sweet morsel for the worms that now thou tramplest upon! Hast thou not seen how loathsome the body is many times in life, by filthy boils and other noisome diseases, and after death what an ugly aspect it has? Forget not the sight that thou sawest once in the churchyard of Dunse, how a body, perhaps sometimes beautiful, was like thin mortar, but much more vile and abominable. The time will come that thou wilt be such thyself.

But what art thou as to thy heart, but a vile, base and ugly thing, so many filthy idols to be found there, like a swarm of the worst of vermin? Art thou not as a cage full of unclean birds! What thoughtest thou of thyself on Monday night, January 16, 1699? What unbelief sawest thou there, what baseness of every kind? And what day goes over thee, but thou seest still something in thee to humble thee? And what wast thou that God has employed in this work? Those that were sometime thy fellows are mean and despised; and wilt thou for all this seek thy own glory? Woe unto thee if thou dost so.

(7) Consider, that 'him that honoureth God, God will honour; but he that despiseth him, shall be lightly esteemed.' *Have respect*, O my soul, with Moses, *to the recompense of reward,* and beware of preferring thy own to the interest of Christ, lest thou be classed among those that seek their own, and not the things of Christ.

(8) Consider what Christ has done for thee. Forget not his goodness, his undeserved goodness to such a base wretch as thou art. Remember him from the land of the Hermonites, and from Mizar-hill; and let love to him predominate in thee, and thou shalt then be helped to sacrifice all to his glory.

*Third, Christ had the good of souls in his eye*. He came to seek and save that which was lost; he came to seek the lost sheep of the house of Israel. So he sent out the apostle to *open the eyes of the*

79

*blind, to turn them from darkness to light, and from the power of Satan unto God.* Follow Christ in this, O my soul, that thou mayst be a fisher of men. When thou studiest thy sermons, let the good of souls be before thee; when thou preachest, let this be thy design, to endeavour to recover lost sheep, to get some brands plucked out of the burning; to get some converted, and brought in to thy Master. Let that be much in thy mind, and be concerned for that, whatever doctrine thou preachest.

Consider, O my soul, for this effect:

(1) What the design of the gospel is. What is it but this? This is the *finis operis;* and if it be not the *finis operantis,* it is very lamentable. It is the everlasting gospel that Christ has made manifest, declaring the will of God concerning the salvation of man.

(2) Consider wherefore God did send thee out. Was it to win a livelihood to thyself? Woe to them that count gain godliness; that will make the gospel merely subservient to their temporal wants. Rather would I perish for want than win bread that way. Well then, was it not to the effect that thou mightst labour to gain souls to Christ? Yea, it was. Have a care then that thou be not like some that go to a place, being sent thither by their master, but forget their errand when they come

there, and trifle away their time in vanity and fooleries.

(3) Consider the worth of souls. If thou remember that, thou canst not but have an eye to their good. The soul is a precious thing which appears if thou consider:

(a) Its noble endowments, adorned with *understanding*, capable to know the highest object; *will* to choose the same; *affections* to pursue after it, to love God, hate sin, in a word, to glorify God here, and to enjoy him here and hereafter.

(b) It must live or die for ever. It shall either enjoy God through all the ages of eternity, or remain in endless torments for evermore.

(c) No worldly gain can counter-balance the loss of it. 'What shall it profit a man, if he should gain the whole world, and lose his own soul? or what shall a man give in exchange for his soul?'

(d) It cost Christ his precious blood ere it could be redeemed. It behoved him to bear the Father's wrath, that the elect should have borne through all eternity; and no less would redeem it. So that the redemption of the soul is indeed precious.

(e) Christ courts the soul. He stands at the door and knocks, to get in. The devil courts it with his baits and allurements. And wilt thou, O my soul, be unconcerned for the good of that which is so much courted by Christ and the devil both? Be ashamed to stand as an unconcerned spectator, lest thou show thyself none of the Bridegroom's friends.

(4) Consider the hazard that souls are in. Oh! alas, the most part are going on in the high way to destruction, and that blindfolded. Endeavour then to draw off the veil. They are as brands in the fire: wilt thou then be so cruel as not to be concerned to pluck them out? If so, thou shalt burn with them, world without end, in the fire of God's vengeance, and the furnace of his wrath, that shall be seven times more hot for unconcerned preachers than others.

(5) Consider what a sad case thou thyself wast in, when Christ concerned himself for thy good. Thou wast going on in the way to hell as blind as a mole; at last Christ opened thine eyes, and let thee see thy hazard, by a preacher (worthy Mr H. Erskine) that was none of the unconcerned Gallios, who spared neither his body, his credit, nor reputation, to gain thee, and the like of thee. And wilt thou preach unconcerned for others? I should abhor myself as the vilest monster, in so doing. Lord, my soul rises at it when I think on it. My soul hates, and loathes that way of preaching: but without thee, I can do nothing. Lord, rather strike me dumb, than suffer me to preach uncon-

cerned for the good of souls; for if dumb, I should murder neither my own soul, nor those of others.

(6) Consider that unconcernedness for the good of souls in preaching, argues:

(a) A dead lifeless heart, a loveless soul, with respect to Christ. If thou hast any life or love to Christ, darest thou be unconcerned in this matter? Nay, sure, he that has life will move; and he that hath love will be concerned for the propagating of Christ's kingdom.

(b) Unbelief of the threatenings of God especially. For if thou believe that the wicked shall be turned into hell, and all the nations that forget God, thou canst not preach to them as if thou wert telling a tale. If thou believe that they must depart into everlasting fire, thy heart will not be so frozen as to be unconcerned for them. The sight of it by faith will thaw thy frozen heart.

(c) A stupid heart, and so a hateful frame. Who would not abhor a watchman that saw the enemy coming on, if he should bid them only in the general provide to resist their enemies, or should tell them that the enemy were coming on, so unconcernedly as they might see he cared not whether they should live or perish? And what a hateful stupidity is it in a preacher of the gospel to be unconcerned for souls, when they are in such hazard?

(7) The devil shames such preachers. He goes about like a roaring lion, seeking whom he may devour; and they, set to keep souls, creep about like a snail. He is in earnest when he tempts; but such are unconcerned whether people hear, or forbear to hear their invitations, reproofs, etc. Yea, how concerned are the devil's ministers that agent his business for him? They will compass sea and land to gain one proselyte. And shall the preachers of the gospel be unconcerned?

(8) If it be so that thou be unconcerned for the good of souls, it seems thou camest not in by the door, but hast broken over the wall, and art but a thief and a robber: 'He that is an hireling, seeth the wolf coming, fleeth, and leaveth the sheep, and the wolf catcheth them' (John 10:1 compared with verse 12); 'The hireling fleeth, because he is a hireling, and careth not for the sheep' (verse 13). O my soul, if at any time thou findest thy heart unconcerned then, not having the good of souls before thee, remember this.

(9) Thou canst not expect God's help, if thou forgettest thy errand. Hast thou not known and experienced that these two, God's help in preaching and a concernedness for the good of souls, have gone with thee *pari passu?* O my soul, then endeavour to be much in following of Christ this way, setting the good of souls before thine eyes;

and if thou dost so, thou mayst be a fisher of men, though thou knowest it not.

*Fourth, Christ had not only the good of souls before his eyes, but he was much affected with their case; it lay heavy on his spirit.* There are these four things wherein this appeared, that occur to me, with which he was much affected.

He had *compassion* on the multitude, because they were as sheep without a shepherd (Matt. 9:36). That the people wanted true pastors, was affecting to him; he had compassion on them. Follow Christ in this, O my soul; pity them that wander as sheep without a shepherd. And let this consideration move thee, when thou goest to preach in planted congregations, where thou wilt even see many that are wandering, though they have faithful pastors. Look on them as sheep not better for them than if they wanted a shepherd. But especially when thou goest to vacant congregations, pity them, commiserate their case, as sheep wanting a shepherd; which no doubt will be a notable means to make thee improve well the little time allowed thee for gathering them in. Be affected with their case; and, for this end, consider:

(1) That such are in a perishing condition: *Where no vision is, the people perish.* They are

ignorant, no wonder, they have none to instruct them; they have lean souls, no wonder, they have none to break the bread of life to them; they wander from God's way, they have none to watch over them, and so the devil takes his opportunity.

(2) Consider that for the most part here at least (this was written while I preached in the presbytery of Stirling) people are deprived of watchmen, in regard of the malignancy and ticklishness of their superiors; so that though the people would ever so gladly receive one to break the bread of life to them, yet they cannot get their will, by reason of these keeping it from them. It would make thy heart to relent if thou sawest a child that would be content to have a pedagogue to guide him, seeing he acknowledges he cannot do it himself, if notwithstanding his tutor should not allow him one, but stand in the way of it, and so the child be lost for want of a pedagogue. So, O my soul, commiserate thou the case of those who would fain have one to watch over their souls, but yet they that should employ their authority, power, wit, etc., to find out one for them, either lie by or oppose the same.

(3) Consider the many souls that go out of time into eternity, during the time that they want a shepherd. They have none to instruct them,

none to let them see their hazard, none to comfort them when death comes, but they slip away, many of them at least, as the brutes that perish. Thou hast found this to have been a cause of thy commiserating such before now, when thou hast spoken to such being a-dying. If this be well considered, and laid to heart, thou canst not but pity them on that very account, which will stir thee up to employ the little time thou hast among them, so as they may be fitted for death.

Christ *wept*, because people in their day did not know, i.e. do, the things that belonged to their peace (Luke 19:41, 42). When he thought upon this their stupidity, it made the tears trickle down his precious cheeks.

O my soul, thou hast this ground of mourning, this day, wherever thou goest. Who are they that are concerned to do what is necessary to be done in order to their peace with God? Few or none are brought in to Christ. It is rare to hear now of a soul converted, but most part are sleeping on in their sins in this their day, like to sit the day of God's patience with them, till patience be turned into fury.

Many heart-melting considerations to this purpose may be found. I shall only say this *in cumulo*, that such a case is most deplorable, in the noontide of the day that people should venture on the feud of such a dreadful enemy as God is, and should sit as quiet even when the sword of vengeance is hanging by a hair over their heads, and notwithstanding that every day may be, for ought I know, their last day, every sermon the last that ever they shall hear, and that ere the next day these enemies shall be made to rencounter with the terrible and dreadful Majesty, who shall go through them as thorns and briers, and burn them up together, by the fire of his wrath, world without end.

O my soul, how canst thou think of this, and not be affected with the case of people as they are now-a-days? Sure, if thou couldst weep, here is ground enough for tears of blood.

He was *grieved* for the hardness of people's hearts (Mark 3:5). It was ground of grief to the Lord Jesus, that people were so hardened that no means used for their amendment would do them good. Follow Christ in this, O my soul; be grieved and affected with the hardness of the hearts of this generation. O what hardness of heart mayst thou see in every corner whither thou goest, and where thou preachest, most part being as unconcerned as the very stones of the wall; and say what thou wilt, either by setting before them alluring promises or dreadful threatenings, yet people are hardened against both, none relenting for what they have done, or concerned about it, though thou wouldst preach till thy eyes leap out.

O happy they whose time God has brought to a period, and taken to himself! Happy servants whom God has called out of the vineyard before the ground grow so hard that almost all labour was in vain! This is a time of mourning for the preachers of the gospel, for people are strangely hardened. Which is the more lamentable, O my soul, if thou consider:

(1) What God has done even for this generation. He has taken off from our necks the yoke of tyranny and arbitrary power, and has given deliverance from Prelatic bondage; and yet for all this the generation is hardened.

(2) How the Lord has been dealing with us by rods. For some time there was great dearth of fodder for beasts; yet that stirred us not up. Afterwards was death of cattle, yet we have not returned to the Lord. Then followed death of men, women and children. He has sent blasting among our corns. This is now, I suppose, the fourth year of our dearth. And for all these things we remain hardened. *O Lord, thou hast stricken them, but they have not grieved; thou hast consumed them, but they refuse to receive correction; they make their faces harder than a rock, they refuse to return.* What shall be the end of such hardness as this?

(3) It is yet more lamentable, in regard the plague of hardness seems to be universal. It is not only the wicked, or openly profane, or those that have no religion, but the professors of religion that are hardened in part. Oh! my soul, this is a day wherein Scotland's pillars are like to fail, a day wherein the hands of our Moses are like to fall, and Amalek is like to prevail.

Many professors desire to hear the causes of God's wrath searched into, but they are not mourning over them; and truly it is most lamentable, that those among us who as so many Joshuas should be discovering the Achans in our camp, that are the troublers of Israel, by a strange kind of dealing are very wary in meddling therewith, or to show them unto people. And it is much to be feared, that there are among us some accursed things that are not yet found out.

O that God would put it in the hearts of Zion's watchmen to discover what these Achans are, and that preachers were obliged even by the church to speak more freely of the sins of the land. But, alas! O Lord, why hast thou hardened all of us from thy fear?

(4) If thou consider, that this hardness of heart is a token of sad things yet to come. *Who hath hardened himself against God, and prospered?* (Job 9:4). Alas! it is a sad prognostic of a further

stroke, that seeing we will not be softened either by word or rod, therefore the Lord will thus do to us; and seeing he will do thus, we may prepare to meet the Lord coming in a way of more severe judgment against us. Sad it is already; many families are in a deplorable condition, and yet nothing bettered by the stroke; and what a sad face will this land have, if it be continued! Spare, O Lord, thine inheritance, thy covenanted people, and make us rather fall on such methods as may procure the removal of the stroke. These, and many other things, O my soul, may indeed make thee grieved for the hardness of this generation.

*Fifth, Christ, was much in prayer*; and that before he preached (Luke 9:18). Follow him in this, O my soul. Thou hast much need to pray before thou preachest. Be busy with God in prayer, when thou art thinking on dealing with the souls of men. Let thy sermons be sermons of many prayers. Well doth prayer become every Christian, but much more a preacher of the gospel. Three things, said Luther, make a divine, *tentatio, meditatio, et precatio*. Be stirred up, O my soul, to this necessary work; and for this end consider:

(1) That thou canst not otherwise say of thy preaching, *Thus saith the Lord*. How wilt thou

get a word from God, if thou do not seek it; and how canst thou seek it but by earnest prayer? If, otherwise, thou mayst get something that is the product of thy empty head to mumble over before the people, and spend a little time with them in the church. But O it is a miserable preaching where the preacher can say, *Thus say I to you,* but no more; and cannot say, *Thus saith the Lord.*

(2) Consider thy own insufficiency and weakness, together with the weight of the work. *Who is sufficient for these things?* which if thou do, thou wilt not dare study without prayer, nor yet pray without study, when God allows thee time for both. It is a weighty work to bring sinners in to Christ, to pluck the brands out of the fire. Hast thou not great need then to be serious with God before you preach?

(3) Consider that word, 'But if they had stood in my counsel, and had caused my people to hear my words, then they should have turned them from their evil way' (Jer. 23:22). There is no doubt that preachers not standing in God's counsel this day, and not making men to hear God's words, is one great reason of the unsuccessfulness of the gospel. Now this way, to wit, prayer in faith, is the most proper expedient for acquaintance with the counsel of God. Neglect it not then, O my soul, but be much in the duty.

Remember, that thou hast found much good of such a practice, and hast found much of the Lord's help both in studying and preaching, by so doing. For which cause thou allottest the Sabbath morning entirely to that exercise, and meditation, if thou canst get it done. Wherefore let this be thy work. And there are these things which thou wouldst specially mind to pray for with respect to this:

(1) That thou mayst have a word from the Lord to deliver unto them; that thou mayst not preach to them the product of thy own wisdom, and that which merely flows from thy reason; for this is poor heartless preaching.

(2) That thy soul may be affected with the case of the people to whom thou preachest. If that be wanting, it will be tongue-preaching, but not heart-preaching.

(3) That thy heart may be inflamed with zeal for the glory of thy Master; that out of love to God, and love to souls thy preaching may flow.

(4) That the Lord may preach it into thy own heart, both when thou studiest and deliverest it. For if this be not, thou shalt be like one that feeds others, but starves himself for hunger; or like a way-mark, that shows the way to men, but never moves a foot itself.

(5) That thou mayst be helped to deliver it

with a suitable frame, thy heart being affected with what thou speakest, faithfully, keeping up nothing that the Lord gives thee, and without confusion of mind, or fear of man.

(6) That thou mayst have bodily strength allowed for the work, that thy indisposition disturb thee not.

(7) That God would countenance thee in the work with his presence and power in ordinances, to make the word spoken a convincing and converting word to them that are out of Christ; a healing word to the broken; confirming to the weak, doubting and staggering ones, etc.; that God himself would drive the fish into the net, when thou spreadest it out. In a word, that thou mayst be helped to approve thyself to God, as a workman that needeth not to be ashamed, rightly dividing the word of truth.

After preaching, Christ was taken up in this work. *And when he had sent the multitudes away, he went up into a mountain apart to pray* (Mark 6:46, Matt. 14:23). Follow Christ in this, O my soul.

It is better to do this, than go away with the great people in the afternoon, which I shun as much as I can; and when at any time I do it, it is a kind of torment to me; which I have shunned, and do resolve to shun more; and if at any time I be necessitated to go, that I shall spend more time alone through grace.

Pray to God, O my soul, that thy labours be not unsuccessful; that what thou hast delivered may not be as water spilt on the ground.

Pray for pardon of thy failings in public duties; and that God may accept of thy mite which thou givest with a willing mind; that he would not withdraw his blessing because of thy failings; but that he would be pleased to water with the dew of heaven the ground wherein thou didst sow the seed, that it may spring up in due time; that the word preached may be as a nail fastened by the Master of assemblies, so as the devil may not be able to draw it out.

Think not, O my soul, that thy work is over, and thou hast no more to do when the people are dismissed. No, no; it is not so. Think with thyself, that the devil was as busy as thou wast, when thou wast preaching; and that afterwards he is not idle. And shall he be working to undo thy work, and thou unconcerned to hold it together? O no, it must not be so; God will not be pleased with this. And alas! I have been too slack in this point before this: Lord, help me to amend.

If a man had a servant that would go out and sow his seed very diligently and faithfully; but would come in, and sit down idle when it is sown, and forget to harrow it and hide it with the earth; would the master be well pleased with him? Yea, would he not be highly displeased, because the fowls would come and pick it up? So, O my soul, if thou shouldst be never so much concerned to get good seed, and never so faithful and diligent in sowing it; yet if after thou turn careless and take not the way to cover it, by serious seeking to the Lord that he may keep it in the hearts of people and make it to prosper, the devil may pick it all up; and where is thy labour then; and how will the Lord be pleased with thee! Therefore pray more frequently, cry more fervently to God, when the public work is over, than thou hast done; and endeavour to be as much concerned when it is over, as when thou wast going to it.

I do not doubt, but many times, when thou preachest, some get checks and convictions of guilt; some perhaps are strengthened; but both impressions wear off very soon. I fear thou must confess, and take with a sinful hand in this, in that thou dost not enough labour to get the seed covered when it is sown, and the nail driven farther in when it is entered.

Though many times thy body is wearied after the public work, yet sure thou mayst do more than thou dost; and if thy soul were more deeply affected, the weariness of body would not be so much in thy mind; but thou wouldst trample on it, that thou might get good done by thy work, and souls might not always thus be robbed by that greedy vulture and roaring lion, the enemy of thy own salvation, and the salvation of others. Although he has been as busy to do harm all the day to souls as thou hast been to do good, yet he will not complain of weariness at night.

Take courage then, O my soul, and be strong in the Lord; and do not give it over to this enemy; endeavour to hold him at the staff's end. Thou hast a good second; Christ is concerned for his own seed as well as thou. Go on then, and be strong in the Lord, and in the power of his might, and let that ravenous fowl never get a grain away as long as thou canst get it kept from him.

Thus then, O my soul, follow Christ, in being taken up in this so necessary an exercise. Thy Lord and Master had no wants to get made up, there was no fear of his failing in this work of the gospel; yet he prayed, to give all, and especially preachers of his word, an example. Lay not aside the pattern then, but write after his copy even in this.

*Sixth, Christ contemned the world.* He slighted it as not meet for any of his followers. He became poor, that we might become rich (Matt. 8:20). He gave himself entirely, at least after his inauguration, to matters that concerned the calling he had to the work of the gospel (John 9:4). All, especially preachers, are to follow Christ in the contempt of the world.

Yet we must beware of imitating him in those things which we are not commanded to follow, as voluntary poverty, this being a part of his satisfaction for the sins of the elect. Neither doth this exempt the preachers of the gospel from a lawful provision of things necessary for themselves, or others they are concerned in; for the apostle tells us, that he is worse than an infidel who doth not provide for his family (1 Tim. 5:8), where churchmen are not excepted.

Yea, it is clear that the ministers of the gospel may sometimes work with their hands for their maintenance, either when the iniquity of the times wherein they live does not allow them what may be for their maintenance, or when the taking of it will hinder the propagation of the gospel, as is clear by the practice of the apostle Paul.

So that that in which, with respect to this, thou art to follow Christ, O my soul, is that thou do not needlessly involve thyself in worldly matters, to the hindrance of the duties of thy calling and station. As thou art a preacher of the gospel, other things must cede and give place to that. This is that which our Lord teaches us: *Follow thou me; and let the dead bury their dead* (Matt. 8:22); and the apostle: *No man that warreth entangleth himself with the affairs of this life* (2 Tim. 2:4). Which was a thing not observed by some, especially our bishops, who acted as magistrates, as well as ministers; a thing which our Lord absolutely refused; *Who made me a judge or a ruler?* says he; yet digested by them, being an infallible sign of their ignorance of the weight of that work. And in my opinion it is not observed either by some ministers now-a-days, who when they have their glebes and stipends sufficient for their maintenance, do notwithstanding take more land a-farming.

For my part, I see not how such can be said not to entangle themselves with the affairs of this life, and go beyond what doth become them as ministers of the gospel. Neither of these are my temptation now, being a probationer. But seeing I am unsettled, a corrupt heart and a subtle devil may take advantage of me, if I be not wary, and by their arguments from my present state may cast me off my feet, if I take not heed.

Therefore, O my soul, beware of preaching smoothly upon the account of getting a call from any parish. Have a care, that the want of that, viz., a call, do not put thee upon men-pleasing. No, no;

that must not be thy business. Remember, God provides for thee even now liberally, as he sees fit. Thou dost not want even so much of the world as is very necessary; and he that has provided for thee hitherto, yea, took thee, and kept thee from the womb, will not forsake thee as long as thou dost not forsake him, but remaineth faithful. Remember, God hath set the bounds of thy habitation, and determined the time. Though men and devils should oppose it, they shall not be able to hinder it. It is God himself that sets the solitary in families; and why shouldst thou go out of God's way to procure such a thing to thyself, or to antedate the time which is appointed of God? Go on in faithfulness, fear not; God can make, yea will make a man's enemies to be his friends, when his ways please the Lord. And though their corruptions disapprove of thy doctrine, and thyself for it, yet their consciences may be made to approve it, and God may bind them up, that they shall not appear against thee.

And what though thou shouldst never be settled in any charge at all? Christ and his apostles were itinerants. If the Lord see it fit, why shouldst thou be against it? If the Lord have something to do with thee in diverse corners of his vineyard, calling thee sometimes to one place, sometimes to another, thou art not to quarrel that.

Perhaps thou mayest do more good that way than otherwise.

If thou hadst been settled at home, then some souls here, which perhaps have got good of thy preaching, would have been deprived of it at least as from thee; and God will always give thee meat as long as he gives thee work; and go where thou wilt, thou canst not go out of thy Father's ground.

Further, if thou shouldst take that way, and transgress for a piece of bread, thou mayst come short of thy expectation for all that, and lose both the world and a good conscience. But suppose thou shouldst by that means gain a call and a good stipend, thou losest a good conscience, which is a continual feast. For how can such a practice be excused from simony, seeing it is *munus a lingua;* and it is a certain symptom that a preacher seeks not them, but theirs; and so thou gettest it, and the curse of God with it. No; Lord, in thy strength, I resolve never to buy ease and wealth at such a dear rate.

Beware, O my soul, that thou close with no call upon the account of stipend. Lay that by when thou considerest the matter. See what clearness thou canst get from the Lord, when any call may be given thee, and walk according to his mind, and the mind of the church. Woe is me if a stipend should be that which should engage me to a place. I would shew myself a wretched creature.

Consider matters then abstracting from that. For surely, this is direct simony; selling the gift of God for money. Let their money perish with themselves that will adventure to do so. Such are buyers and sellers, that God will put out of his temple. Such are mere hirelings, working for wages; and too much of Balaam's temper is to be found there.

That will provoke God to curse your blessings, and to send a moth among that which thou mayst get; and it surely will provoke God to send leanness to thy soul, as he did with the Israelites in the wilderness, when he gave them what they were seeking.

Thou canst not expect God's blessing on thy labours, but rather that thou shouldst be a plague to a people whom you so join with. In a word, thou wouldst go in the wrong way, and be discountenanced of God, when you have undertaken the charge.

There is yet a third case wherein this contempt of slighting of the world should appear in one sent to preach the gospel; that is, when a man is settled, and has encouragement or stipend coming in to him, and so must needs have worldly business done, especially if he be not single, whereby he is involved in more trouble thereabouts, than any in my circumstances for the time are. In such a case a minister would endeavour to meddle as little as he can with these things, but shun them as much as lies in him, especially if he have any to whom he can well trust the management of his affairs. For surely the making of bargains or pursuing them are not the fit object of a minister's employment. Not that I mean simply a man may not do that, and yet be a fisher of men; but that many times the man that takes such trouble in the things of the world to catch them, indisposes himself for the art of man-fishing. But this not being my case, I pass it, referring any rules in this case how to walk till the Lord be pleased so to tryst me, if ever. Only do thou, O my soul, follow Christ in the contempt of the world. Do not regard it. Thou mayst use it as a staff in thine hand, but not as a burden on thy back, otherwise the care of souls will not be much in thy heart.

And to help thee to this contempt of the world, consider the vanity of the world. Solomon knew well what it was to have abundance, yet he calls *all vanity of vanities, all is but vanity.* The world is a very empty thing, it cannot comfort the soul under distress. No; the body it can do not good to when sore diseases do afflict it. The world cannot profit a man in the day of wrath. When God arises to plead with a person, his riches avail nothing. When he lies down on a deathbed, they can give him no comfort, though all his coffers were full. When he stands before the tribunal of God, they profit him nothing. Why then should such a useless and vain thing be esteemed?

Consider that the love of the world, where it predominates, is a sign of want of love to God: *If any man love the world, the love of the Father is not in him.* Yea, even in a gracious soul, in so far as the love of the world sways the heart, in so far doth the love of God decay. They are as the scales of the balance, as the one goes up, the other goes down.

Consider the uncertainty of worldly things. They are as a bird that takes the wings of the morning, and flees away. Set not thy heart then on that which is not. How many and various changes as to the outward state are in a man's life. The beggar may well say, *Hodie mihi, cras tibi.* Men sometimes vile are exalted, honourable men are depressed; and the world is indeed *volubilis rota*; that part which is now up, shall ere long be down. Seest thou not that there is no constancy to be observed in the world, save a *constant inconstancy*! All things go on in a constant course of vicissitude. Nebuchadnezzar in one hour is walking with an uplifted heart in his palace, saying, *Is not this great Babylon that I have built, etc.?* and the next driven from men, and made to eat grass as an ox. Herod in great pomp makes an oration, the people cry out, *It is the voice of a god, and not of a man,* and he is immediately eaten up of worms. The rich man today fares sumptuously on earth, and tomorrow cannot get a drop of water to cool his tongue.

Consider the danger that people are in by worldly things, when they have more than daily bread. The rich man in Luke 12 felt this to be a stumbling-block on which he broke his neck. The young man in the gospel, for love of what he had of the world, parted with Christ, heaven and glory, and so made a sad exchange. Prosperity in the world is a dangerous thing; it is that which *destroys fools* (Prov. 1:32). When Jeshurun waxed fat, he kicked against God, and forgat the Lord that fed him (Deut. 32:15). It was better for David when he was on the one side of the hill, and his enemies on the other, and so in great danger, than when he was walking at ease on his house-top, when he espied Bathsheba. And of this, O my soul, thou hast had the experience.

Our Lord tells us, that it is very hard for a rich man to be saved; and teaches us that it is hard to have riches and not set the heart on them. What care and toil do men take to themselves to get them! What anxiety are they exercised with, and how do they torment themselves to keep them! And when they are got and kept, all is not *operae pretium* to them. Many by riches and honour, etc., have lost their bodies, and more have lost their souls. It exposes men to be the object of others, as Naboth was even for his vineyard; and *who can stand before envy*? (Prov. 27:4; See also 1 Tim. 6:9, 10). This ruined Naboth (1 Kgs. 21) *Da ebolum Belisario, quem virtus extulit, invidia depressit.* So that he that handles the world, can very hardly come away with clean fingers. It is a snake in the bosom that, if God prevent it not by his grace, may sting thy soul to death.

Remember the shortness and the uncertainty of thy time. Thou art a tenant at will, and knowest not how soon thou mayst remove; and thou canst carry nothing with thee. Therefore having food and raiment (which the Lord does not let thee want), be therewith content (1 Tim. 6:7, 8). Thou art a stranger in this earth, going home to thy Father's house, where there will be no need of such things as the world affords. Why shouldst thou then, O my soul, desire any more than will carry thee to thy journey's end? Art thou going to set up thy tent on this side of Jordan to dwell here? Art thou saying, It is good for me to be here? Art thou so well entertained abroad, that thou desirest not to go home? No, no. Well then, O my soul, gird up the loins of thy mind. Thou art making homeward, and thy Father bids thee run and make haste: go then, and take no burden on thy back; lest it make thee halt by the way, and the doors be shut ere thou reachest home, and so thou lie without through the long night of eternity.

And to shut up all, remember that there are other things for thee to set thy affections on than the things of this world. There are things above that merit thy affections. Where is Christ, heaven and glory, when thou lookest upon the world, highly esteeming it? Seest thou no beauty in it to ravish thy heart? Surely the more thou seest in him, the less thou wilt see in the world.

And hath not experience confirmed this to thee? Alas, when the *beauty* of the upper house is in my offer, that ever I should have any kindness for the world, that vile dwarf and monster, that shall at the last be seen by me all in a fire. *Sursum cor,* O my soul! thou lookest too low. Behold the King in his glory; look to him that died for thee, to save thee from this present evil world. See him sitting at the right hand of the throne of the Majesty in heaven. Behold the crown in his hand to give thee, when thou hast overcome the world. Behold the recompense of reward bought to thee with his precious blood, if thou overcome.

Ah! art thou looking after toys, and going off thy way to gather the stones of the brook, when thou art running for a crown of gold, yea more than the finest gold? Does this become a man in his right wits? Yea, does it not rather argue madness, and a more than brutish stupidity? The brutes look down, but men are to look up. They have a soul capable of higher things than what the world affords: therefore,

*Pronaque cum spectent animalia caetera terram,*
*Os homini sublime dedit, caelumque tueri*
*Jussit, et erectos ad sidera tollere vultus.*

Be then of a more noble spirit than the earth-worms. Let the swine feed on husks. Be thou of a more sublime spirit: trample on those things that are below. Art thou clothed with the sun? Get the moon under thy feet then; despise it, look not on it with love, turn from it, and pass away.

Let it not move thee if thou be poor, Christ had not where to lay his head.

Let not the prospect of future troublesome times make thee solicitous how to be carried through; for 'thou shalt not be ashamed in the evil days, and in the days of famine thou shalt be satisfied'. God hath said it (Ps. 37:19), therefore do thou believe it.

Be not anxious about thy provision for old age, for by all appearance thou wilt never see it. It is more than probable thou wilt be sooner at thy journey's end. The body is weak; it is even stepping down to salute corruption as its mother, ere it has well entered the hall of the world: thy tabernacle pins seem to be drawing out by little and little already. Courage then, O my soul; ere long the devil, and the world, and the flesh shall be bruised under thy feet; and thou shalt be received into eternal mansions.

But though the Lord should lengthen out thy days to old age, he that brought thee into life will not forsake thee then either. If he give thee life, he will give thee meat. Keep a loose hold of the world then; contemn it if thou wouldst be a fisher of men.

*Seventh, Christ was useful to souls in his private converse*, taking occasion to instruct, rebuke, etc., from such things as offered. Thus he dealt with this woman of Samaria. He took occasion from the water she was drawing to tell her of the living water, etc. Thus being at a feast, he rebuked the Pharisees that chose the uppermost seats, instructing them in the right way of behaviour at feasts.

O my soul, follow Christ in this. Be edifying

in your private converse. When you are at any time in company, let something that smells of heaven drop from your lips. Where any are faulty, reprove them as prudently as you can. If they appear to be ignorant, instruct them when need requires, etc. And learn that heavenly chemistry of extracting some spiritual thing out of earthly things. To this purpose and for this end endeavour after a heavenly frame, which will, as is storied of the philosopher's stone, turn every metal into gold. When the soul is heavenly, it will even scrape jewels out of a dunghill. Whatever the discourse is, it will afford some useful thing or another.

Alas, my soul, that you follow this example so little! O what a shame is it for you to sit down in company, and rise again, and part with them, and never a word of Christ to be heard where you are. Be ashamed of this, and remember what Christ